What Is Beautiful?
Published by Parent Cue

5870 Charlotte Lane, Suite 300
Cumming, GA 30040 U.S.A.

Other Parent Cue products are available online and direct
from the publisher. Visit our website at www.TheParentCue.org
for more resources like these.

ISBN: 978-1-63570-100-5

©2020 Abbie Smith Sprunger

Authors: Abbie Smith Sprunger
Illustrations: Ashley Lauren Snyder
Design Editor: Hannah Crosby
Editor: Karen Wilson
Director of Publishing: Mike Jeffries
Project Manager: Nate Brandt

Printed in the United States of America

First Edition 2020

1 2 3 4 5 6 7 8 9 10

08/01/20

WHAT IS BEAUTIFUL?

To Ana Marie & Aaliya Nöel,
your beauty astounds me,
and I could not love you more.
— Abbie

To Margo Moon,
may you always be
YOU to the FULL
— Ashley

"What is beautiful?", I wonder. "And when can it start? Does it have a certain size and certain colored parts?"

Such meaningful questions, my precious child,
with marvelous answers, full of lovely and wild.

Beauty isn't always tidy, nor contained in a box.
It may sparkle from the sky, or a tall stack of rocks.

It begins with to

an invitation quite simple,

unrelated to a mirror
or the depth of one's dimple.

are the gem that God has designed,
made to create, to bloom and to shine.

is to feel, to laugh and to cry,
to hope and to rest, to live kind and alive.

To awaken true beauty,
then, you must only

BE
YOU

Be YOU

TO THE
FULL

child, ever being made new.

Unique and magnificent is that fullness of you,
God's canvas of which there can never be two.

He dreamed up your body, the width of your nose,
your shape and your wonder, your teeth and your toes.

Your fingers and freckles, God knows every one,
your fears and your dreams, the way that you run.

Your parts that are squishy, and those that make sounds,
to Him they're a delight, your beauty astounds.

The strands of your hair,
the scabs on your knees,
all thoughts that you think,
He already sees.

He knows the length of your legs,
the shade of your skin,
the sound of your laugh,
the curve of your chin.

There is no mistake on that body of yours,
created to breathe,
to grow and to soar.

You're brave and creative,
made just as you are,
to love and be loved,
in every longing and scar.

Nothing to prove, no need to perform,

you're fully delighted-in since the day you were born.

To answer your question—
"What is beautiful?", then, just

TO THE FULL

For beautiful is what you've always been.

Abbie (Smith) Sprunger is the author of multiple books, but makes her debut in children's books with What Is Beautiful? As a proud mother of daughters, one of whom is adopted from India, these pages are personal in a quotidian sense. Similarly important is Abbie's choice to give $1 of every What Is Beautiful? sale toward research preventing mother—to—child HIV transmission.

Abbie is a graduate of Emory University ('03) and Talbot Seminary's Institute for Spiritual Formation ('09) and lives and works alongside her husband, Micah, as caretakers of Wesley Gardens Retreat in Savannah, Georgia. Abbie is the proud mother of Elliana, Eden and Aaliya. Given the differences of ethnicity in their home, and raising two daughters, these pages run personal. Abbie's story holds lengthy seasons trapped in eating disorders and exercise addictions. Her journey of healing and discovering beauty are reflected in this prose. You can follow Abbie at @wesleygardenslife.

In an effort to bridge readers' voices to awareness and proactivity, Abbie is also partnering with the ONE Campaign, a global movement against extreme poverty and preventable diseases. Please add your voice at ONE.org!

Ashley Lauren Snyder is an interior designer by trade, turned artist by passion. She's wife to Jacob and Mama to Margo Moon, with a "why" in life of knowing God and making Him known, walking through days with her palms up and heart open. Ashley dreams big, and smiles bigger.

You can find her at @ashleylaurensnyder, where she shares her heart and life (probably on the back porch with a cup of coffee) from their cabin nestled in the Ozarks of Arkansas.